15
PROBLEMS

15
ELIMINATIONS

15
SOLUTIONS

TO FIX THE
AMERICAN PUBLIC SCHOOL
SYSTEM

By Vern "Mr. V" Vilmenay

Self published
ISBN: 0615430899
ISBN 13: 9780615430898

For information, please contact:

Vern "Mr. V" Vilmenay
P.O. BOX 904
Woodland Hills
CA 91365
Printed in the United States of America

PREFACE

There are two reasons why I decided to write this book.

The first is responsibility. I sincerely believe that each one of us is living on this earth to make or create something to better the world we live in. We are here for a purpose. We need to think about replacing what we have been taking, such as the physical, mental, moral, and monetary aspects around us. After all, if the people who came before us didn't leave anything, where would that leave us? There wouldn't be anything for people to learn and improve upon. Where would all the professionals be? Think about Bill Gates, the President, Wal-Mart, our teachers, and doctors, the list is endless. All these people/companies have improved products and ideas that have made our lives easier.

The second reason for writing this book is that our country is failing in its education system. We need to get back to basics.

For over 36 years, I have been a Martial Arts practitioner and teacher, and have taught many students of all ages, from children to adults. Throughout my life as a Martial Artist, many mentors and teachers have inspired and helped me become who I am today. Fortunately, I have been able to pass on this wisdom to all of my students. While operating my own studio, in West Hills, California, thousands of students have come before me together with their parents. I have been privy to many discussions regarding the schooling system in this country, and whether it is or isn't as affective as it should be.

Are students getting the best education America has to offer?

Personally I don't think so, and I am sure there are many out there that feel and have the same views as me.

I don't know if people recognize the value and influence a great teacher can have. Throughout my teaching career, my students would tell me what an impact I was having on their lives. Being a great teacher is the ultimate result, but you have to have the proper ingredients to make this happen. All teachers and parents deserve respect and recognition for being good at what they do.

Why do we applaud and praise reality TV Shows, materialism, and bad behavior?

It all sells! All of it makes better news and better viewing!

This must change!

We must applaud and praise the people and things that matter in this world!

As a reminder, in case you have forgotten, the three most important people in our lives and our children's lives are:

Good parents, who nurture, guide and give balance to their children.

Good teachers, who guide and help build strong, inquisitive minds.

Good doctors, who help their patients, maintain a healthy body and a healthy mind.

I would like to share with you my three biggest role models:

Martin Luther King,
a prominent leader in the African American civil rights movement. He was an iconic figure in the advancement of civil rights in the United States and around the world, using nonviolent methods following the teachings of Mahatma Gandhi.

Mother Teresa,
a humanitarian and advocate for the poor and helpless.

Mahatma Gandhi,
political and spiritual leader of India, he deployed satyagraha, which is non-violence resistance during the Indian independence movement. Gandhi led nationwide campaigns to ease poverty, expand women's rights, build religious and ethnic peace, and increase economic self-reliance.

They were all givers, leaders, and teachers.

"STOP TAKING, START GIVING"

CONTENTS

This book is very easy to follow.

SECTION ONE

Top 15 Problems

The Top 15 Problems

1. Board of Directors

2. Too Many Teachers

3. Electronics/Computers

4. Dress Code for Teachers and Students

5. Parents

6. Dead Subjects

7. Hours

8. Salaries/Money

9. Testing

10. Respect

11. Budgets

12. Vacations

13. Class size

14. Punishments

15. Grades

SECTION TWO

Top 15 Eliminations

The Top 15 Eliminations

1. All Board Members and their staff. There are too many Chiefs and too many Indians. Who will ultimately make the decisions?

2. Ban tenure for teachers. We all know what happens when one gets everything one wants, one usually gets lazy and eventually lacks motivation to improve.

3. Eliminate cell phones. Are we communicating with space or with people?
   Why are people's brains less efficient these days?
   Why are computers doing all the homework and school work for us?
   We need to increase our brainpower, not diminish it.

4. Respectable school attire should be worn by all teachers and students.
   If we don't act like professionals, how can we produce them?

5. Parents, why are you complaining so much? Why do you want someone else to raise your children for you? Why did you have them in the first place? Get involved!

6. Why are so many dead and boring subjects being taught in our schools today?
   Let's clean up our yards.

7. Are we running a marathon? The school hours are too long for both students and teachers.

8.   Besides our parents, who is the next most influential person in our lives?
      Our teachers, "Hello!" So, why are we paying our teachers PEANUTS?
      At this rate we may as well call them "SNOOPY" not "TEACHERS"

9.   Why are we willing to judge our kids progress based on one score on a single test?

10.   What ever happened to RESPECT?
      "RESPECT FOOL" Yes, the song Aretha Franklin sang. Need I say more?

11.   What Budget? As long as I get my fat check, I just don't care…I'm alright Jack!

12.   Was I supposed to do that? Sorry, I didn't have time, I was on vacation again!

13.   "Oh say can you hear me? Can you see me"? No, classes are too big. I need binoculars and a blow horn.

14.   You can't punish me, my mommy and daddy will kick your asses, then you'll be sorry!

15.   If I don't get straight A'sses, that's not my fault, it's my computers fault!

"ELIMINATION IS THE NEW BEGINNING"

SECTION THREE

Top 15 Solutions

The Top 15 Solutions

1 THE BOARD OF DIRECTORS

We currently have school boards, with people who primarily work for the state and the city, who to date, haven't been able to execute a good job for the school system. These people come from differing professions and none from an educational work background. None of them know each other; they don't know the schools, the teachers or the students and their parents. Yet they are making major decisions for our schools, now that's what I call crazy!!

There is something very wrong with this picture in my mind.

Why are all these people being paid all this money with fringe benefits and pensions?

These people need to be out!

Why are we not employing educational professionals who understand the system, the needs and wants of the teachers and students, and ultimately what the children should be learning?

The solution to the problem is TO ELIMINATE ALL the board members now. Hire a successful local businessperson who is not interested or wants compensation, is neutral in his decision making, and will be able to do the job without prejudice. As a Chairman, this person will be responsible for only one school in their district. They would hire and develop a team for each school. These teams would consist of a CEO, CFO, and COO, and they will be the decision makers regarding the hiring and firing of teachers.

The teams will have training in public relations in order for them to be able to hire qualified people within the organization.

A year-to-year contract will be issued, with responsibilities to manage, listen, and keep on budget. (Don't cross the red line please,) we want to see the books in the black. At the end of each year, there will be an assessment on each individual. If too much money is spent and the school is declining in its performance, then they are fired. If the school has improved and they are in the black, then the contract is renewed!

Some of our local business leaders will also be invited to the schools to donate their free time as Evaluation Members, such as lawyers, doctors and other businessmen or women. Their input would be very beneficial. These would be people who are very successful in their careers, who do not need or want to be paid, but who actually care about our schools and the community. They will help to evaluate each teacher and they will help decide which contract is renewed.

Periodically, each teacher will be responsible to go to one of the local businesses, relevant to the subject they are teaching, for their continuing education. For example; a math teacher will go to a CPA office, a science teacher will visit a laboratory etc.

HOW TO COME UP WITH EXTRA CASH NEEDED TO FUND THIS PROGRAM:

1. Sell old, inoperable schools.

2. Sell old fire departments, buildings, and vacant lots.

3. Open a school pro-shop for uniforms and supplies.

4. Reduce the amount of libraries being built, remember, people use computers for research much more than they use libraries.

5. Eliminate all the "Dead Subjects" as mentioned before.

6. Set up an Alumni program – Donation for each school.

7. Charge a fee for parking at the schools. All teachers and executives to be exempt from paying.

8. Fund raising within the schools. (Parent volunteers)

9. Good money management and more.

10. Take the school public. Each parent and student can own shares in their school, in their investment. *(note: Parents can purchase shares on behalf of their children)*. The schools can only go public if they are making money. Part of the revenue the schools are currently receiving, is coming from tax dollars from each state.

"THERE CAN ONLY BE SOLUTIONS, IF YOU SOLVE THE PROBLEMS"

2 TEACHERS.

All teachers should be on a year-to-year contract. We all know what happens when someone becomes too comfortable in his or her job, laziness sets in, they start running on autopilot and the students get bored. This leads to lack of motivation and apathy on both sides. Not good! How can you be self-motivated to perform when you have a lifetime contract that guarantees you a paycheck no matter how bad you do your job? Don't misunderstand me, I believe that all teachers should get a good salary based on the subject they're teaching. Some of the required knowledge needed would be in communication, motivation, language/arts, reading, and of course teaching skills. They need to be an expert in their subject and they need to be good! They need to earn it.

We would offer a job advancement program, teacher training and continuing education. Our program will provide an incremental salaries bonus, benefits, and a retirement plan.

In order to manage this, we have to eliminate the tenure program, replace it with a year-to-year contract. Teachers will have a good starting base salary and opportunity for promotion.

I really believe we would start attracting great, young, professional teachers if they know they will not be overworked, underpaid, disrespected and be able to provide a great life for their families.

The funding for this would come from all the money that is being saved by getting rid of all the peripheral Board Members and only keeping in place the people needed.

(see, Board of Directors)

Let's develop an Academic Award for the teachers, the schools and the people running them. Awards can be given for "Best Teacher" in the field of Math, Science and Language/Arts, "Best School" and for "Best CEO, CFO, and COO".

Lastly, an award can be given to "School of the Year".

Let's make a big deal about Education, Teachers, and the Staff.

"GOOD TEACHERS HELP CREATE GOOD MINDS"

3 ELECTRONICS AND COMPUTERS.

Ban all cell phones, iPods'/radios and computers in schools, for all students. How can you concentrate if you are texting? It has been widely published that it is dangerous to text while driving…why….because it causes lack of concentration!!

At school, you should be improving your mind not the agility of your fingers on a phone.

It is true, electronic gadgets have done a great deal for the good of mankind; however, it has made people lazy, both physically and mentally. These days, no one can think without using Google, cell phones or just asking someone else to think for them.

In the old days, one had to know how to conduct research without using a computer and solve math problems without using a calculator. To get good grades, one had to study using books and not copying from a computer. These days, everyone seems to be getting A's but they don't know Jack.

People across the board are becoming too lazy to learn. There is too much reliance on computers, which is affecting the ability of conducting basic research. It is too easy to cheat using a computer. Most students are able to download information from a computer and then claim it as their own. Homework is no longer accomplished with paper and pencil anymore, let alone trying to use our minds for simple calculations. We use the internet for everything. When the students have research assignments they go straight to a computer, and as if by magic, the answers to the questions appear.

Students are receiving straight A's but can't even spell "kat".

This is all due to misusing the computer in a classroom.

We need to eliminate the use of computers in classrooms. All teachers and students should be able to do the class work by memory. Let's get back to basics. It is better to get a solid "C" then a lousy "A". If both student and teacher were doing their work without gadgets doing the thinking for them, we would start creating better minds, which would in turn lead to future teachers, scientists and doctors – THE THREE MOST IMPORTANT PROFESSIONS IN OUR LIVES.

We need to be able to start building and creating things again. We have so many computers, yet we have a lousy economy. You cannot create jobs out of nothing. These days, everyone wants to work with computers so they can sit on their ass all day doing nothing. We have many web browsers, yet we do not have enough jobs for people to work. Why? Because we are not building or creating anything. Everybody complains about illegal immigrants, but they are the ones that go out and find work. Why? Because they don't mind getting their hands dirty and being creative by building tangible things.

The President cannot create jobs, no matter how much the government barks, they are depending on all our tax dollars for their salaries. "HELLO?" The Economy will only prosper if we are being productive and creative, like manufacturing goods, building houses, roads etc. Do you know what I mean? We have to stop concentrating just on computers. After all, one of the wealthiest men in the United States, Warren Buffett, only buys things he can touch and feel. Buffett's Omaha-based company owns clothing, insurance, furniture, utility, jewelry, corporate jet companies, and See's candies.

So, let's start teaching our children how to think on their own, ban electronics in the classroom.

"ELECTRONICS WERE CREATED BY THE CONTENT OF ONES MIND"

4 DRESSCODE.

Okay, here we go, let's hear it people, I am destroying your morality, your children's rights are being infringed on and their self-esteem is being crushed. If we want our children to become better citizens, more productive in the classroom and be prepared so they can compete in the business world, remember, it all starts in the home and in the classroom.

We need to adopt a uniform system for all schools now.

Most professions have a uniform code. Look at the Army, Navy, Marines, Astronauts, Martial Arts, Doctors and Nurses, need I go on? They don't have low self esteem because they wear uniforms, they wear them because they are practical and it helps us recognize who they are.

So, why don't our schools adopt this system? It would make life so much easier on the parents if you think about it. No more fighting about which clothes are appropriate for school and which ones aren't! No more wasting money on designer clothes for the kids to show off at school! No more peer pressure!

This is not just for the students, but the teachers must also dress like professionals. They must wear business attire, including a necktie for men and no tennis shoes. Remember people, it's all about self-respect and discipline.

All schools will be able to design their own crest or logo, which can be embroidered on to the uniform or worn as a patch. An American manufacturer can be contracted to make all the uniforms and patches. A pro shop can be set up in each school, the uniforms can be purchased by the parents at the beginning of school, and replacements can be bought throughout the year. These shops can be run by the students, and this would help them be productive while learning basic working skills.

Guess what? Our schools will benefit from the profits made.

Lastly, we will be bringing manufacturing jobs back to America.

God bless our uniforms.

The style and design should be the same for all schools, with the only difference being the color. Each school can adopt their own school colors.

For example:

Girls	**Boys**
Khaki skirt just below the knee	Long khaki pants
Light blue polyester/cotton blouse	Light blue short sleeve shirts
Black, 1-inch heel shoes	Tie
Khaki 'V' neck sweater	Khaki 'V' neck sweater

"A UNIFORM MAKES A PERSON,
SO DRESS FOR SUCCESS"

5 PARENTS

I have listened to a lot of parents in the past, most complaining how bad the school system is, how bad the teachers are, how bad the state and the city are, but I have never heard them OFFER A SOLUTION TO THE PROBLEM. All they do is talk, talk and talk! Last time I checked, too much talking never accomplished anything, except frustration.

Therefore, I say stop talking and complaining and get involved. How? Simple. Help in the classrooms, volunteer for the PFA, (Parent Faculty Association), donate your time, help with homework, be aware of exactly what it is your children are learning, and where the information is coming from.

I understand there are many parents who work during the day. These parents do not get to see their children until the evening. They can still be involved, they can ask their child questions about their day, find out what work they have brought home and if it has been completed. It is OK to look inside their backpack occasionally! Believe me; children want their parents to be involved.

If a computer is being used at home, parents have a responsibility to ensure that its use is monitored, no cheating while getting information together. Children need help in understanding the importance of doing their own work and not copying from the computer. To be successful students, parents must make sure their children are using their minds to do their work and not relying on computers to do the thinking for them.

If you suspect there's a problem, contact the school. Find out before it's too late. Teachers cannot work in isolation; they also need feedback from parents, that's what makes them successful and excellent teachers, and that's what makes an excellent school.

"GREAT PARENTS, GREAT KIDS. GREAT KIDS COME FROM GREAT PARENTS."

6 DEAD SUBJECTS

Most of our children have a hard time spelling the name of the subjects they're learning, so why are we wasting funds, time, and energy teaching obsolete subjects which will not be useful in the business world.

I will explain to you why some of these classes should be retired from the curriculum. By eliminating these classes we will free up cash in order to pay our teachers and executives better salaries, so they can do a much better job managing and teaching.

ART All of the famous artists were never wealthy while they were alive. They were all self- taught. Let's give the kids some crayons; let's save money; let's help our teachers be more productive.

P.E. Another dead subject. It is a lot less expensive, and to no expense to the state, if kids are enrolled in Martial Arts, baseball, basketball or football. These activities take place after school hours; children will still get the physical activity they need to lead a healthy life. Don't forget, they still have recess and lunch at school, and during these times the kids are also being physical; so don't worry, they won't be leading a sedentary life style. However, it will be up to the parents to ensure that their kids take up these activities outside of school, and if money is an issue for them, there are parks where the kids, together with their parents, can go and be active!

FOREIGN LANGAUGES. I was under the impression that we want everyone to speak English. Well, "no más Español por favor." We need to save money. Eliminate our Spanish classes and introduce more Language/Arts classes. This will enable us to have fewer students in each classroom, so teachers can pay more attention to each student. This makes for excellent teaching, and that is what we need.

French, like Spanish, "Parlez vous Française?", "AU REVOIS", bien, bien. We just reduced the students in our Math class.

MUSIC. Children who are interested in this subject have radios, iPods', cell phones, etc. They're up to date. Kids that are born with a musical talent can pursue music outside of school; there are plenty of music stores offering lessons at discounted prices. Believe me, if the parents recognize that their child has talent, they'll make sure their kid is found by the right agents.

There are some classes currently taught that just don't make sense.

Jesse Jackson wanted black children to start learning "EBONICS". The term *Ebonics* (a blend of *ebony* and *phonics*) gained recognition in 1996 because of the Oakland School Board's use of the term in its proposal to use African American English in teaching Standard English in the Oakland Schools. Jackson said that they were looking for tools to teach black children standard English so they might be competitive. GIVE ME A BREAK!

We want people to speak proper English, we want the illegal immigrants to learn English, yet we are teaching foreign languages. Let's concentrate on teaching and learning English. Learn other languages from Rosetta Stone.

Our goal is to save millions of dollars and ultimately lower class sizes.

We need to start teaching finance, business studies, economics, science, money management. Did you notice I didn't mention computer studies; a four year old can navigate his way around a computer. Computers do not create jobs to the masses, only to a few billionaires.

We need architects to help re-design and re-build our schools, roads and bridges.

We need engineers to help design better structures.

We need better teachers to help our school system.

We need better scientists to help improve our lives.

We need better leaders like Martin Luther King, Bill Gates, Warren Buffet, Mother Teresa, and Gandhi.

We need leaders who care about the world, not the pure profits.

"DEAD SUBJECT, DEAD MINDS"

7 HOURS

What are we doing? Running a marathon in our classrooms? The hours are too long.

Since we are eliminating a bunch of worthless classes, we should break the hours into shifts, six days a week, one hour a day and one subject a day. School would be open 11 months a year, with 1 month vacation for all. This schedule will eliminate boredom in the classroom, everyone will be able to retain what they have learned that day and it will eliminate all that homework children bring home everyday. Teachers, parents, and students will have less stress and be more content.

PROPOSED SCHEDULE

GRADES	**HOURS**	**DAYS PER WEEK**
Kindergarten	Eliminate	Should be with parents
1 & 2	12pm to 1pm	3
3 & 4	1pm to2 pm	3
5 & 6	2pm 3pm	4
7 & 8	3pm to 4pm	5
9 & 10	9am to 11am	6
Lunch time	11am to 11:55am	6

The purpose for this proposed schedule is to eliminate over crowding in schools and over crowded classrooms.

Teachers would teach one subject per day, all of the 11th and 12th Graders would be able to work part time for work experience.

Now that we have eliminated some classes, we will be able to add classes that are more practical. Most 11th and 12th Graders have a good idea what it is they want to do once they leave high school and go out into the world.

We should have business people from different fields, come, and teach some classes. We could offer local businesses tax incentives in order for them to provide internships for all 11th and 12th graders based on their chosen future professions. All Saturday classes would be hands on training in business and finance.

"LESS HOURS, LESS STRESS,
GREAT MINDS"

8 MONEY, MONEY, MONEEEY.

As far as I'm concerned, the most important professionals on this earth are teachers, scientists, and doctors.

Why are entertainers being paid more money than teachers, scientists, and doctors?

I am dumbfounded.

As we have talked about earlier on in this book, teachers should be on a year-to-year contract. We need to start with a base salary for all teachers, with salary increments beginning at 2% and rising to 6%. These advancements would be based on experience, the difficulty of the subject being taught, class participation, grade results and enthusiasm.

We need to create titles for all teachers in order to promote from within. This would help in attracting excellent teachers. In order for senior teachers to keep their jobs, they would have to further their education and take a test every year in order to get a renewed contract. By doing this, bad teachers can be eliminated and good teachers retained.

Salary and opportunity is the key.

Now, as far as benefits, teachers will be charged a set fee for insurance, and like the Motion Picture Association, we can start an Education Hospital Association (E.H.A) for all educators.

We should create a self-managed pension plan. If an educator starts a Roth Ira, we would provide them with a matching percentage, paid from excess funds at the end of the fiscal year. However, if your school is out of budget, then none for you, if your school is in the black, enjoy your summer vacation. Of course, all these proposals would be based on the level of management, teaching standards, grades, and savings.

In other words, you must earn it!

"STOP SPENDING, START SAVING, START PLANNING"

9 TESTING

All students in the U.S are tested way too much. They spend weeks and months getting ready for tests. Teachers today, have no time to be creative, therefore, teaching and learning is no longer fun!

Not everything that is important in a child's education can be evaluated by a test.

How can tests show us the student's ability to find alternative explanations to problems, to raise questions, to dig further into areas that interest them, and to be creative thinkers. They can't!

A student's success must not be based on one single, multiple choice test score, which has been marked by a machine. Politicians say it's cheap!

Is that how they view the future of our society, as CHEAP?

Athletes such as basketball, baseball, or football players are assessed based on their season's performance; they are NOT assessed in a randomly chosen week of the season, based on one game.

So, why are we willing to treat our kids that way?

Throughout my teaching career, I have promoted many students with higher belts. Over time, the students need to demonstrate an improvement and understanding of the techniques taught at each level. By assessing the students this way, I was able to determine their strengths and weaknesses, and then correct them accordingly. Each student is an individual, each student learns in a different way. You have to be able to determine those factors to be able to help the child succeed. Once I knew the student was ready for their next belt level, I then allowed them to test.

How can a machine do this? Oh, I forgot, let's use it because it's cheap!

A multiple-choice test, scored by a machine, can give a quick reflection of student performance, but it does not show the overall picture. Student assessment must be judged in other areas such as research papers, essays, research projects etc. As well as test results, a teachers evaluation of the student must be submitted together with a students past performance.

Let's invest a little more time and energy on our students so they can achieve excellent and true results based on their overall efforts.

The success of our future society depends on our children being innovative, inquisitive, and possessing imagination, not by deciding whether an answer is A, B, C or D.

"HUMAN INTERVENTION IS OUR ROAD TO SUCCESS"

10 RESPECT

How do we expect to have good, effective teachers when the students and parents have no respect for them?

How many times have you heard parents complaining about how hard it is and how stressful their lives are looking after two or three children? Well, a teacher has to look after a lot more than two or three! In elementary school, they have to teach up to 30 or more in a small classroom, and middle school teachers are expected to teach and get to know in excess of 150 students. Now, that is hard stressful work!

We want our teachers to be proud of their job. They need to get the respect they deserve. Any student or parent who disrespects any teacher should be suspended from school for a minimum of two weeks.

Have you ever heard of anyone messing with the IRS? No, because they know the consequences. With that being said, remember respect goes both ways. A teacher should also respect their students and the students' parents. If they should show any disrespect they will also be suspended for a two-week period without pay.

"ONE WITHOUT SELF-RESPECT, HAS NO RESPECT FOR OTHERS"

11 BUDGETS

How in the world could someone sitting somewhere in an office in a cubicle, manage to balance the budget for the whole school system?!!! I don't know, do you?

Most of those people are just doing a job. They are number crunching. They have never visited the schools, met the teachers, parents or students. They have never asked a pertinent question.

My solution to this problem is to give the school, the responsibility of controlling their own budget. At the start of the fiscal year, the budget is given to the school, and the responsibility goes to the CEO and his/her staff. As we stated before, if they do a good job, they should stay in the black, if they don't, their contract will not be renewed.

If each school is managed like Wal-Mart or a McDonald franchise, and there is an opportunity for bonuses and advancement, there wouldn't be any problem attracting some excellent teachers and CEO's.

I am talking from experience. I have managed several small businesses, over a span of 30 years. I've been able to stay in the black year after year, without using credit or taking out bank loans. So you see, it can be done. (Ask Dave Ramsey).

"WITHOUT BUDGETING WISELY, YOU'LL NEVER SPEND WISELY"

12 VACATION

There is too much time wasted on taking extra days off. What are we learning?

"NADA". Spanish for nothing.

Every major corporation trains their staff on how to manage, sell, hire and fire people, and balance budgets. All this training must be implemented in the school system.

By not taking all these extra days off, we can utilize that extra time for something a lot more productive.

We want our partners in the teaching business to do well. We need to train them so they understand what is expected of them and that they do it well.

When the Lakers or the Raiders go and compete, they are never without a game plan. So, let's plan to WIN. Let's lead by example.

Let's teach our teachers, to teach our children.

"REJUVENATING THE MIND IS GOOD FOR THE BODY, ABUSING THE SYSTEM IS TIRING"

13 CLASSROOMS

Teaching and learning should be fun! There should be energy in the classroom from both teacher and student. Everyone needs to be enthusiastic, and of course, the subject relevant!

The teacher's job is to get the children involved in the subject that is being taught.

Active learning is better than passive learning. If kids are being lectured to for hours, it will lead to excruciating boredom! Let the kid's brainstorm a problem together, let them discover the answer and not just tell them what is written in a book.

If active discussions are held, students encouraged to speak out, giving their opinions, debating, then every student can shine, be creative, be better thinkers and doers and not followers.

We have to teach our staff how to be excellent teachers, how to get children involved in the subject. There are people born with the gift of teaching; they have to help others master these special skills. Our children are bored and tired due to long hours and poor teaching abilities.

As the great Bruce Lee once said; "You may learn from him, but his way is not the only way."

Another suggestion to learning is to have all classes conducted without textbooks.

The student would study and complete the assigned homework with the use of a textbook.

In class the next day, the subject studied for homework can then be discussed in class between student and teacher, without the use of a textbook. The teacher would know immediately if the student had not done their homework.

This method will prepare students for test taking; the childrens self-esteem will be improved, and they will develop better memory retention.

However, homework must be kept to a minimum.

Too much homework DOES NOT MAKE YOU SMARTER.

Wording in textbooks must be improved. When children ask their parents for help with a homework question, because the wording is so awkward, the parent has no understanding of what the question is asking for. Teachers often have to refer to their answer books to comprehend the meaning of some questions in textbooks. How can we help our children with their work, if the text in books is unintelligible?

Throughout this book, emphasis and examples have been given on how to decrease class sizes. Classrooms would become more manageable and teachers would be able to be more involved with each student. This would lead to a better understanding of each student's strengths and weaknesses and the teacher would not have to use *"blow horns"* or *"binoculars"* to communicate with our children.

"LECTURES ARE BORING, DEBATES ARE EXCITING"

14 PUNISHMENT

Everyone including the CEO and their staff, teachers, students and parents should be held accountable for their behavior, period.

- If the CEO does not manage properly, he or she should be fired.

- If a teacher does not teach well, he or she shouldn't have their contract renewed.

- If a student doesn't do their homework, then they should be suspended from that class for the day.

- If a student shows up for school out of uniform, they should be sent home immediately.

- If a parent disrespects a teacher, then their child should be suspended for the day.

- If a parent doesn't volunteer to assist the classroom at least once a month, they should be fined $100 for each month they don't help.

Rules have to be followed. The IRS fines us for late payments, the banks fine us for late payments, traffic violations are given if you drive incorrectly, court marshaled in the military, impeached in the government.

So why should our schools not follow rules? They should!

We have rules for everything; the rules are there to keep order and peace in society. Everyone needs to get involved.

Teachers, are not the only ones to blame when the system goes wrong, everyone is accountable.

"PUNISHMENT DEVELOPS CHARACTER"

15 GRADES

What are grades? As far as I'm concerned, grades were designed to collect our tax dollars, just like social security numbers, driver's license numbers, or any other numbers that have been created and linked to a person.

There is so much emphasis put on an A, B, C, D, or F.

Who came up with the definition for each grade?

- A = The ultimate.
- B = Get back.
- C = You are lame.
- D = Wasn't good.
- F = Get in the doghouse.

Man oh man, we don't judge our children based on their ability anymore. I know many people who have received straight A's at school. They grew up to be an ass and the guy we put in the doghouse is now hiring them.

As we all know, some people have great memory retention skills and are very good at memorizing testing material that they have downloaded from a computer. They achieve an "A" grade, and shortly afterwards it's all forgotten. We idolize the person with an "A" grade, and punish the person who has studied hard but only received a "B" or a "C".

I know quite a few people who have received straight "A's" and like I said before, they are probably the dumbest people I know, have no common sense and I'm sure some of them are running the school system now. That's probably why it is in such a mess.

I would rather employ the person who received an "F", who has common sense and work ethic to run our school system.

"JUDGE ME BY MY ABILITY AND NOT BY 'A' LETTER"

EPILOGUE

"WHO CARES?"

- When some people are not getting the proper education, ***"WE ALL SHOULD"***

- When living in the suburbs, your children start emulating and applying all the negativity they see and hear, ***"WE ALL SHOULD"***

- When you have to go to the urban area, people see your nice fancy car, your sparkling jewelry, ***"WE ALL SHOULD"***

- When you go to the airport, located in the ghetto, and you have to drive solo, ***"WE ALL SHOULD"***

- When the train lines start connecting the urban area to the suburbs, ***"WE ALL SHOULD"***

- When your children cannot fill out a job application form, ***"YOU SHOULD"***

- When your children cannot find an entry level job, ***"YOU SHOULD"***

- When graffiti is replacing your landscaping, ***"YOU SHOULD"***

- When your children don't have a belt to hold their pants up, ***"YOU SHOULD"***

- When your children don't have a best friend to bond with, ***"YOU SHOULD"***

- When the rich are getting richer, and you are getting poorer, ***"YOU SHOULD"***

- When you cannot afford health care, ***"YOU SHOULD"***

- When your children's hair do's are braids and Mohawks, ***"YOU SHOULD"***

- When your teenage daughters are getting pregnant, ***"YOU SHOULD"***

- When your teenage daughters are dressing like 'hoochie mamas', ***"YOU SHOULD"***

- When your children are getting abducted, assaulted, raped or murdered, ***"WE ALL SHOULD"***

- When you and your children are having a better relationship with the cell phone and computer, ***"YOU SHOULD"***

- When your children are committing suicide, overdosing on drugs, stealing, lying, cheating, ***"YOU SHOULD"***

- When your children would rather talk to strangers than talk to you, ***"YOU SHOULD"***

- When your children prefer eating at fast food restaurants than having a family meal at home, ***"YOU SHOULD"***

- When we have no leaders to look up to, we think we are better than other human beings. We don't know how to pray, say please, say thank you, open the door for someone, be kind, be compassionate, we have no pride, no morals.

"WE ALL SHOULD CARE"

CONCLUSION

I have kept this book brief and to the point. My aim is to get the point across, quickly and effectively. Our school system is inefficient, some teachers are not very good and our students are suffering. Our children are the future. Action needs to be taken.

There have been and are a lot of critics who can serve a list as long as my arm, and maybe longer, with the problems of the American Public School System today, but I have yet to see them come up with any kind of solution to this growing list.

This short and concise book is the solution to the top 15 problems as I see them!

Great education is the key to developing children into influential, successful adults.

GREAT PARENTS   —   GREAT KIDS

GREAT KIDS   —   GREAT PARENTS

GREAT TEACHERS   —   GREAT STUDENTS

GREAT STUDENTS   —   GREAT MINDS

GREAT MINDS   —   GREAT FUTURE

GREAT FUTURE   —   GREAT EDUCATION

GREAT EDUCATION   —   GREAT SCHOOLS

GOD CREATED   —   DOCTORS MAINTAIN

DOCTORS MAINTAIN   —   GOD SAVES

GOD SAVES   —   GOD IS

ACKNOWLEDGEMENTS

I would like to thank all the teachers who have given themselves without recognition. To all the doctors who made house calls to save someone and who have never received an "Academy Award" for it. To all of our heroes, all over the world, who are dead or alive, who have made it possible for us to continue learning and living well. Last, but not least, to all the givers who gave without expecting anything in return.

This book is dedicated to you!

"PERSERVERANCE REQUIRES DISCIPLINE"